W9-AET-239

THE ASSASSINATION OF JOHN F. KENNEDY

BY PETER BENOIT

CHILDREN'S PRESS®
An Imprint of Scholastic Inc.
New York Toronto London Auckland Sydney
Mexico City New Delhi Hong Kong
Danbury, Connecticut

Content Consultant
James Marten, PhD
Professor and Chair, History Department
Marquette University
Milwaukee, Wisconsin

Library of Congress Cataloging-in-Publication Data
Benoit, Peter, 1955–
The Assassination of John F. Kennedy / by Peter Benoit.
pages cm.—(Cornerstones of freedom)
Includes bibliographical references and index.
ISBN 978-0-531-28200-7 (lib. bdg.) — ISBN 978-0-531-27665-5 (pbk.)
1. Kennedy, John F. (John Fitzgerald), 1917–1963—Assassination—
Juvenile literature. I. Title.
E842.9.B447 2013
973.922092—dc23 2013000100

Printed in the United States of America 113

1 2 3 4 5 6 7 8 9 10 R 23 22 21 20 19 18 17 16 15 14

Photographs © 2014: Alamy Images: 12 (incamerastock), 32, 57 (Mug Shot), 4 top, 14 (Pictorial Press Ltd); AP Images: 15 (Charles Dharapak), 10 (HB), 54 (Wilfredo Lee), cover, 16, 28, 34, 39, 51; Corbis Images: 13, 25, 50, 58 (Bettmann), 41 (Pete Fisher/Bettmann), 4 bottom, 7, 36, 56 bottom; Everett Collection/CSU Archives: 8, 47, 59; Getty Images: 22 (Art Rickerby/Time Life Pictures), back cover (Carl Mydans/Time Life Pictures), 24 (CBS Photo Archive), 45 (Dan Farrell/NY Daily News Archive), 55 (Dirck Halstead/Time Life Pictures), 40 (Fotosearch), 2, 3 (Keystone), 20, 29 (Mondadori), 35 (Terry Ashe/Time Life Pictures), 5 bottom (Time Life Pictures/National Archives), 48 (Time Life Pictures/National Archives), 38 (Tom Williams/CQ-Roll Call Group); Superstock, Inc./Everett Collection: 5 top, 11, 19, 23, 30, 31, 44, 56 top; The Granger Collection: 26 (Rue des Archives), 42; The Image Works/Atlas Archive: 6; The Sixth Floor Museum At Dealey Plaza: 49.

Maps by XNR Productions, Inc.

Did you know that studying history can be fun?
BRING HISTORY TO LIFE by becoming a history investigator. Examine the evidence (primary and secondary source materials); cross-examine the people and witnesses. Take a look at what was happening at the time—but be careful! What happened years ago might suddenly become incredibly interesting and change the way you think!

Contents

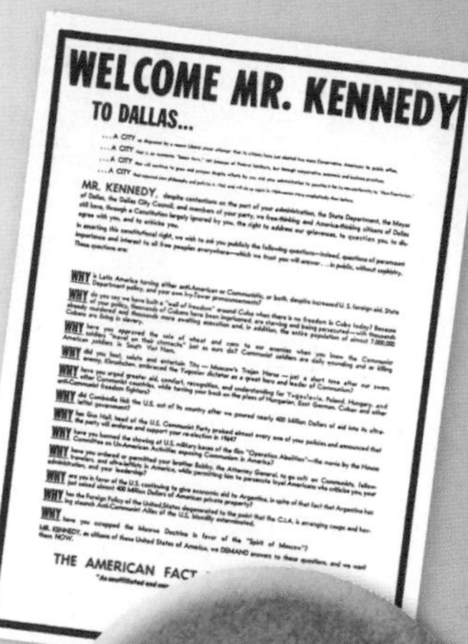

WELCOME MR. KENNEDY
TO DALLAS...

SETTING THE SCENE

A Trip to Dallas

President Kennedy signed the order that created the Peace Corps on March 1, 1961.

In November 1963, John F. Kennedy had been serving as president of the United States for nearly three years. He had created the Peace Corps to improve the lives of people in less developed countries. He successfully avoided war with the Soviet Union during the Cuban missile crisis of 1962. However, he had also struggled to accomplish many of his most important objectives, such

AT AGE 43, KENNEDY WAS THE YOUNGEST

as addressing the issue of civil rights. Many Americans were unhappy with Kennedy's leadership.

In June 1963, the president had addressed the nation about his intention to support and expand equal opportunities for African Americans. The speech angered many whites in the South. With the 1964 presidential election less than one year away, Kennedy understood that he would need to win over southern voters to stand a chance at reelection. He and his advisers determined that a personal appearance in Dallas, Texas, could help persuade people to vote for him.

President Kennedy's remarks about the civil rights struggle in the South created controversy among white southerners.

PERSON EVER ELECTED PRESIDENT.

CHAPTER 1

THE UNIMAGINABLE

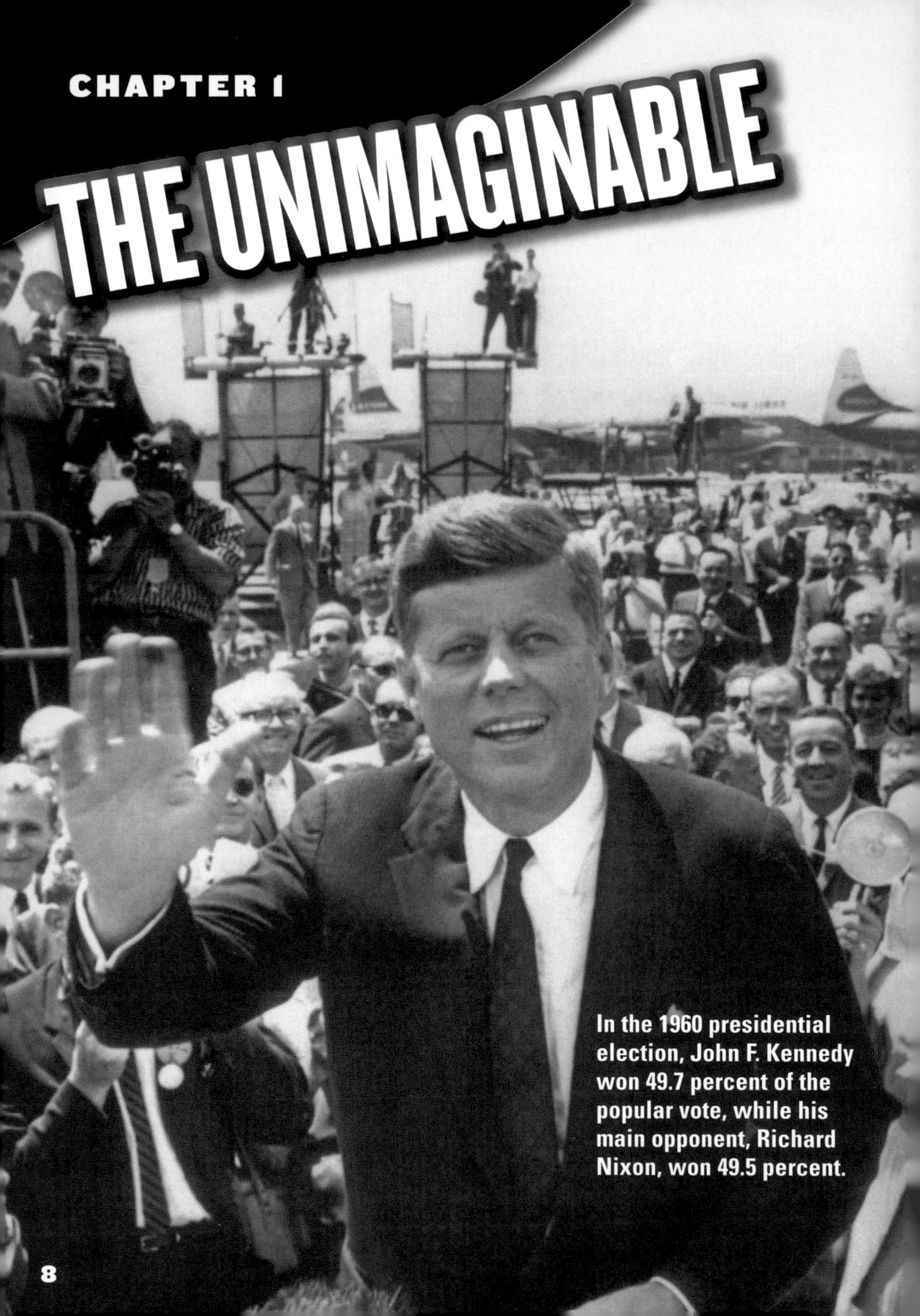

In the 1960 presidential election, John F. Kennedy won 49.7 percent of the popular vote, while his main opponent, Richard Nixon, won 49.5 percent.

PLANS FOR THE UPCOMING 1964 election were never far from President Kennedy's thoughts. Kennedy's 1960 election victory was the closest of the 20th century. He had an especially difficult time in Texas. He had narrowly won the state's votes despite having Texas senator Lyndon Johnson as his running mate. In Dallas, one of the state's largest cities, Kennedy had received fewer votes than his opponent, Richard Nixon.

After President Kennedy's death, Kenneth O'Donnell (right) went on to work with President Lyndon Johnson and manage the presidential campaign of Kennedy's brother Robert.

Planning the Trip

After the 1960 election, opposition to Kennedy in Dallas had grown more vocal. Many people believed he was too soft on **communism**. With the rise of such opposition, Kennedy would face an even more difficult time getting votes in Texas in the 1964 election than he had in 1960. A trip to meet with citizens and lawmakers in Dallas could help win some voters back over to his side.

Kennedy's special assistant, Kenneth O'Donnell, knew the president would never agree to meeting only with local lawmakers and business people in Dallas. Kennedy looked forward to meeting average citizens and having them see him. O'Donnell, the Secret Service, and Texas governor John Connally kept this in mind as they worked out the details of the president's trip.

After months of planning, O'Donnell and Connally finalized Kennedy's appearance at the Dallas Trade Mart a week before his arrival. There, Kennedy was scheduled to speak before a crowd of 2,600 enthusiastic supporters.

The route for the presidential **motorcade** was then set. Kennedy's motorcade would leave from Dallas's Love Field airport and travel on Main Street through suburban neighborhoods. However, Main Street did not connect directly to the

YESTERDAY'S HEADLINES

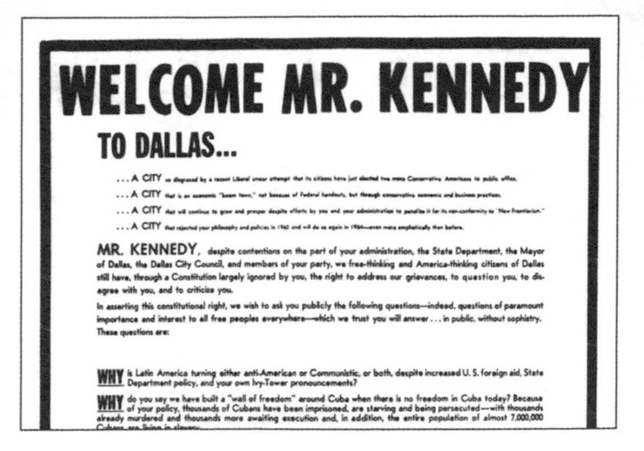

WELCOME MR. KENNEDY

TO DALLAS...

...A CITY

...A CITY

...A CITY

...A CITY

MR. KENNEDY, despite contentions on the part of your administration, the State Department, the Mayor of Dallas, the Dallas City Council, and members of your party, we free-thinking and America-thinking citizens of Dallas still have, through a Constitution largely ignored by you, the right to address our grievances, to question you, to disagree with you, and to criticize you.

In asserting this constitutional right, we wish to ask you publicly the following questions—indeed, questions of paramount importance and interest to all free peoples everywhere—which we trust you will answer . . . in public, without sophistry. These questions are:

WHY is Latin America turning either anti-American or Communistic, or both, despite increased U. S. foreign aid, State Department policy, and your own Ivy-Tower pronouncements?

WHY do you say we have built a "wall of freedom" around Cuba when there is no freedom in Cuba today? Because of your policy, thousands of Cubans have been imprisoned, are starving and being persecuted—with thousands already murdered and thousands more awaiting execution and, in addition, the entire population of almost 7,000,000

The day President Kennedy was scheduled to visit Dallas, the *Dallas Morning News* printed an announcement from a group called the American Fact-Finding Committee. The announcement attacked Kennedy's foreign policy, claiming that he was aiding communism's spread in foreign countries. It also promised that Dallas would vote against him in the coming election. The announcement perfectly illustrates the difficulties Kennedy would likely have faced in 1964 had he lived to campaign for a second term as president.

Stemmons Freeway, which led to the trade mart. Instead, the motorcade would turn onto Houston Street at the end of Main, and then onto Elm Street. It would pass along Dealey Plaza on Elm Street before exiting onto the Stemmons Freeway. The Texas School Book Depository stood at the corner of Houston and Elm. The route through Dealey Plaza would make Kennedy easily visible to the public but would also make it easier for potential enemies to get close.

After the 10-mile (16-kilometer) route was finalized, Secret Service agents Winston Lawson and Forrest Sorrels met with Dallas police chief Jesse Curry to discuss their security plans and arrange for the president's police protection. Though the route itself

The Texas School Book Depository is now home to a museum devoted to President Kennedy.

Until Kennedy's assassination, it was common for presidents to be highly visible when riding in a motorcade.

raised concerns, the presidential limousine was designed with security in mind. The car, named SS-100-X by the Secret Service, was a customized 1961 Lincoln Continental convertible.

A FIRSTHAND LOOK AT THE MOTORCADE'S ROUTE

On November 19, 1963, the *Dallas Times Herald* announced the route of Kennedy's motorcade. Two days later, it also printed a map. The announcements increased spectator turnout but also posed a further security risk to the president. See page 60 for a link to view the *Herald*'s announcement of the route online.

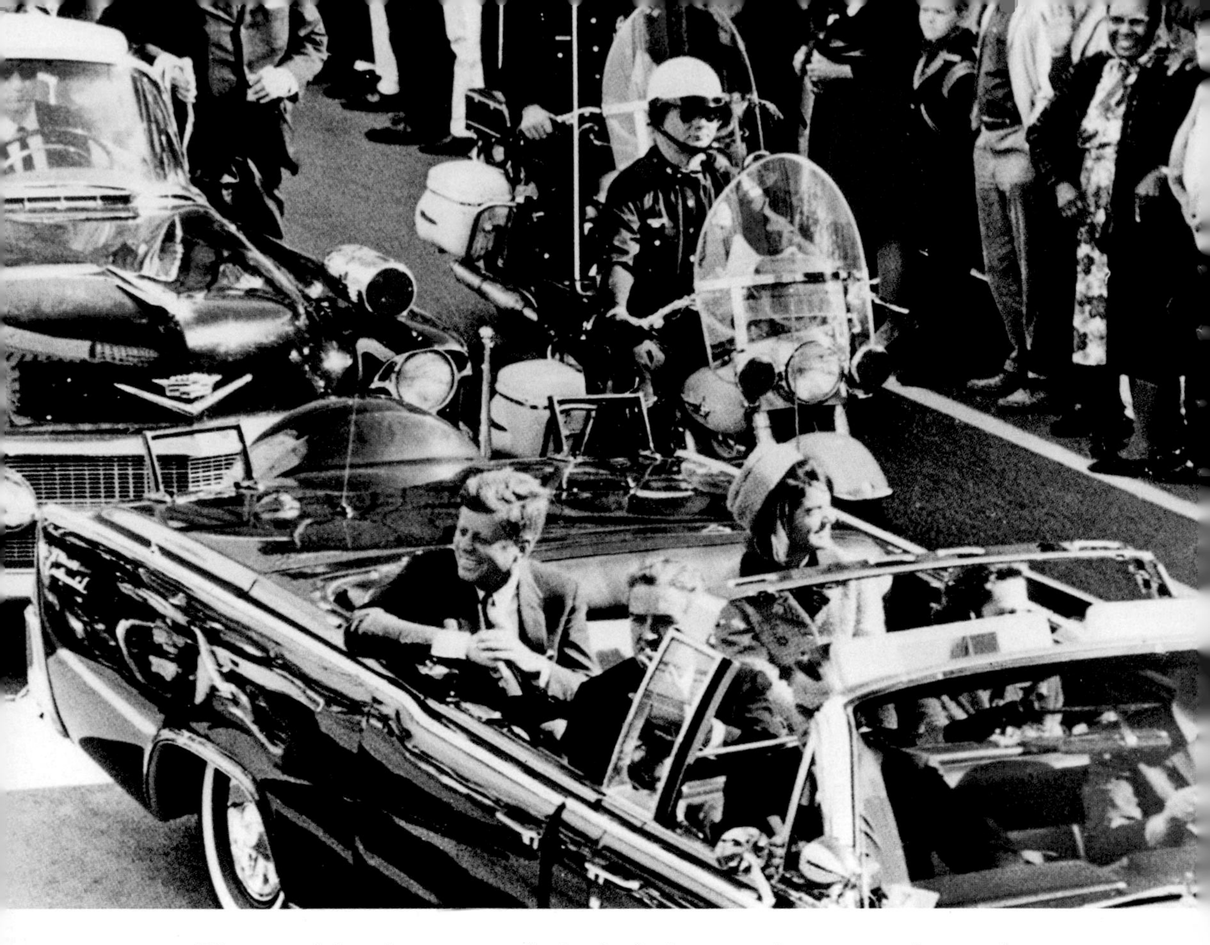

The president's motorcade included several motorcycles and cars full of police and Secret Service agents.

The SS-100-X had been lengthened to 21 feet 8 inches (6.6 meters) and outfitted with heavy armor. It had retractable side running boards where agents protecting the president could ride. However, Kennedy disliked the running boards and did not allow agents to ride on them. The back bumper had an additional two places for agents to stand. The trunk was fitted with handgrips for their safety. However, as the motorcade prepared to begin its route on the morning of November 22, 1963, Kennedy waved the agents off when they tried to board. He wanted a clear view of the people when he looked back.

On the Move

By 11:55 a.m. central standard time (CST), the motorcade began to roll away from Love Field. A white car, followed by six Dallas policemen on motorcycles, scouted the route a quarter mile ahead. Police chief Jesse Curry followed them in an unmarked white police car. Riding with him were agents Lawson and Sorrels and a Dallas sheriff. The SS-100-X followed five car lengths behind Curry's vehicle. Kennedy and his wife, Jacqueline, rode in the backseat. Governor Connally and his wife, Nellie, sat in the seat directly in front of them. Four motorcycle escorts rode alongside SS-100-X. A Secret Service vehicle packed with agents followed a car length behind. Following

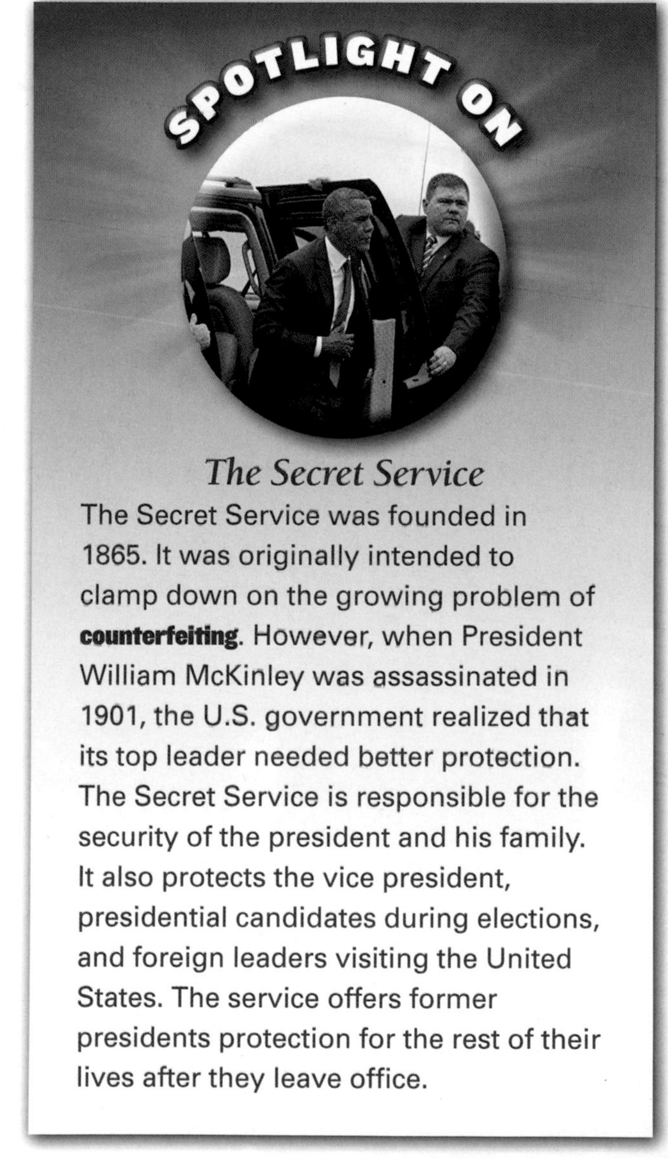

The Secret Service

The Secret Service was founded in 1865. It was originally intended to clamp down on the growing problem of **counterfeiting**. However, when President William McKinley was assassinated in 1901, the U.S. government realized that its top leader needed better protection. The Secret Service is responsible for the security of the president and his family. It also protects the vice president, presidential candidates during elections, and foreign leaders visiting the United States. The service offers former presidents protection for the rest of their lives after they leave office.

them, Vice President Johnson's limousine was trailed by another Secret Service car. At the rear were press cars, more motorcycle escorts, a staff car, and a car carrying the president's doctor, George Burkley.

The day was sunny, and the temperature was a comfortable 65 degrees Fahrenheit (18 degrees Celsius). Ten minutes into the journey, Kennedy told his driver to stop when he saw a man holding a sign asking the president for a handshake. People a block away saw that the motorcade had stopped, and they flocked to the car.

Huge crowds swarmed the route to catch a glimpse of President Kennedy as his motorcade drove through Dallas.

Kennedy asked the driver to stop again a few blocks later so he could greet a nun and several small children. Chief Curry realized that he had badly underestimated the turnout for Kennedy's visit. By 12:23 p.m., the presidential motorcade had slowed to a crawl on Main Street. Tens of thousands of people cheered for the president and first lady, who smiled and waved to the crowd. Nellie Connally turned to the president and remarked that the people of Dallas loved him.

The SS-100-X turned onto Elm Street shortly before 12:30. Spectator Charles Brehm had brought his five-year-old son, Joe, to Dealey Plaza to see the president. Brehm ran across the lawn, set Joe down, and told the boy to wave when the president's car passed. Three workers gazed wide-eyed from the fifth-floor corner window of the nearby Texas School Book Depository. People standing across the street waiting for the motorcade saw the workers. They also saw a slender, brown-haired man crouching in the window directly above them. He seemed to be distracted.

Shots Fired

The crowd began to roar, and applause grew louder as the motorcade approached Dealey Plaza. Though the plaza was not as packed as Main Street had been, the crowd was equally vocal in support of Kennedy. The president waved to the adoring crowd, and then brushed his hair back from his face. Nearby, a Kennedy supporter named Abraham Zapruder began to film the procession through Dealey Plaza. The clock atop the book depository read 12:30.

Suddenly, a loud crack broke through the noise in the plaza. Most people looked around, confused by the sound. Governor Connally, an avid hunter, instantly recognized the unmistakable noise of a rifle firing. He turned his head toward the sound's source and found himself looking at the book depository. A man named James Worrell, standing directly in front of the building, looked up and saw a gun barrel sticking out from the sixth-floor window.

Three seconds later, the crack of the sniper's rifle again echoed across the plaza. Charles Brehm, less than 20 feet (6 m) from the president, watched as Kennedy raised his hands to his throat. Special Agent Clint Hill leapt from the running board of the following car and sprinted toward SS-100-X. Special Agent Roy Kellerman, riding in the front seat of the limousine, turned to see Kennedy clutching his throat and Connally slumped over in distress. Both men had been shot.

As Agent Hill reached for the handrail on the trunk of the presidential limousine, he heard another shot strike Kennedy's head. Kellerman had quickly issued an order to speed to Parkland Memorial Hospital after the president and governor were hit, but the third shot had struck the president before the driver could get the car out of harm's way.

Abraham Zapruder watched in horror, certain Kennedy was already dead. Charles Brehm threw himself on top of his son to protect him. By now, press photographers and a television cameraman had seen the sniper pull his rifle back into the book depository's window.

Witnesses dropped to the ground when they heard the shots fired from the book depository.

Chief Curry shouted into his radio to alert Parkland Memorial that SS-100-X would arrive in a few minutes. The plaza was filled with terrified, screaming people. The crowd scrambled, not knowing if the sniper would fire again. Officer Marrion Baker, believing that the shots had come from the book depository roof, entered the building and sprinted up the northwest stairwell. When he reached the second floor landing, he saw a man walking away from him. The building superintendent identified him as an employee named Lee Oswald. Baker barely paused, continuing to the roof instead. Oswald used the opportunity to escape.

CHAPTER 2

SEARCHING FOR A KILLER

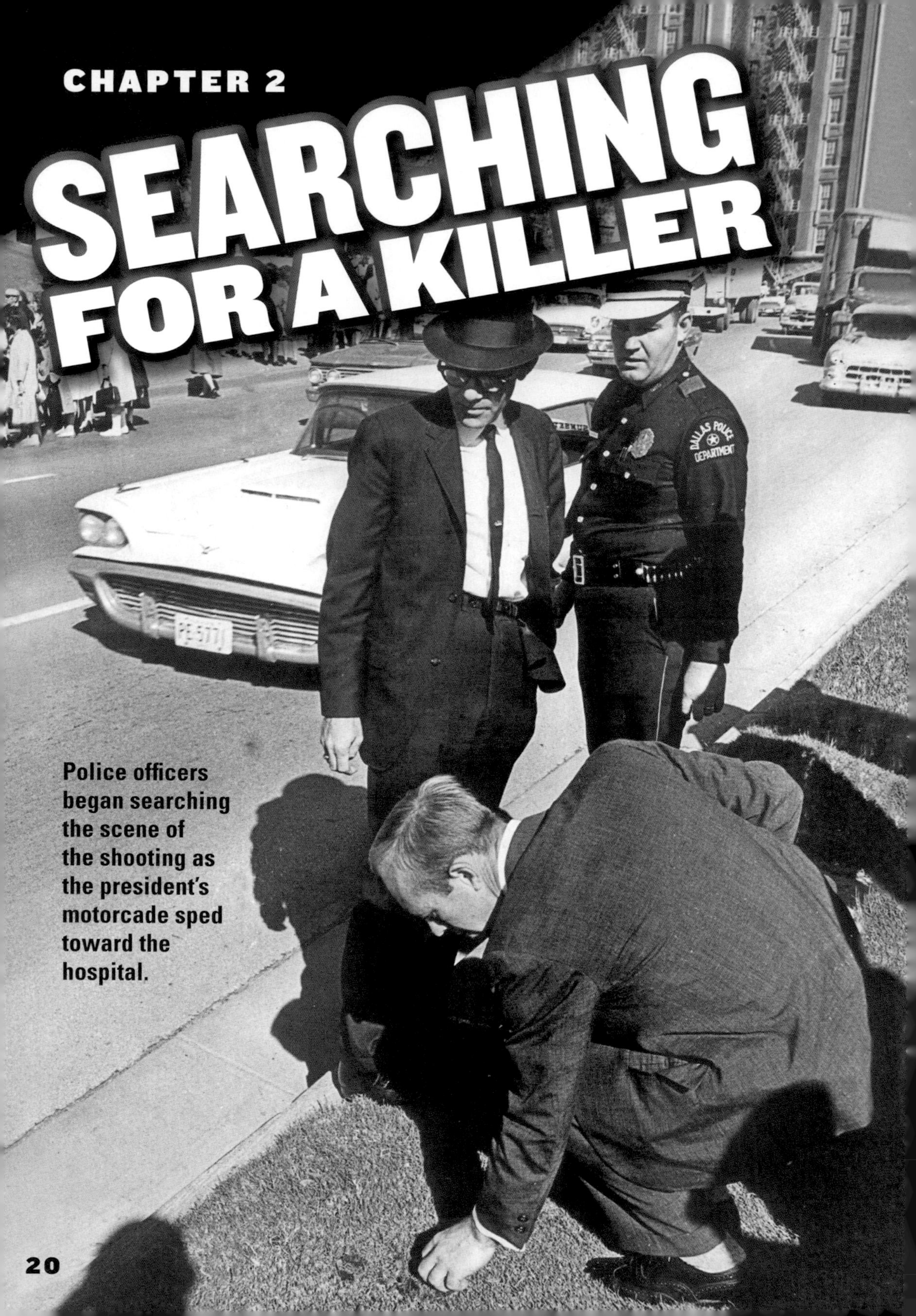

Police officers began searching the scene of the shooting as the president's motorcade sped toward the hospital.

THE MOTORCADE RACED against the clock as it sped along the Stemmons Freeway. Jacqueline Kennedy sobbed uncontrollably over her seemingly lifeless husband. Nellie Connally took some comfort in her unconscious husband's trembling hand. She told him, "It's going to be all right." The motorcade exited the freeway and rocketed past the trade mart where Kennedy was to have spoken, and then made a sharp turn toward Parkland Memorial Hospital. The motorcycle escorts accelerated uphill, hit a slope at the side of a railroad, and went airborne. Landing hard, they immediately leaned left. Sparks flew as their kickstands scraped the roadway. The limousine's tires squealed a few feet behind them. Parkland Memorial Hospital was now less than a mile away. Seconds later, SS-100-X arrived at the emergency entrance.

Police and Secret Service agents guarded the area as the president's car parked in the hospital's ambulance entrance.

Medical Attention

Agent Kellerman quickly stepped from the car and took command. He ordered other agents to bring a **gurney** immediately and prepare to move Kennedy. Agent Dave Powers raced to the side of the limousine and saw the first lady covered in blood. The president's eyes were fixed in a motionless stare. Governor Connally groaned. Secret Service agents and a Dallas police officer placed Connally on a gurney and wheeled him into the hospital. The remaining agents turned their attention to the president. In shock, the first lady did not want them to remove her husband from the car, but the agents finally convinced her. She watched the agents load Kennedy's body on a gurney and race toward the emergency room. At around the same time, news services passed along details of the shootings to television and radio stations. The tragic news quickly spread around the world.

Dr. Charles Carrico was the first to encounter Kennedy when he was wheeled into the trauma room. The president had no pulse and only a faint heartbeat. He was losing massive amounts of blood, and his complexion had become bluish white. Kennedy labored for breath, and his eyes were unmoving. Dr. Carrico immediately inserted

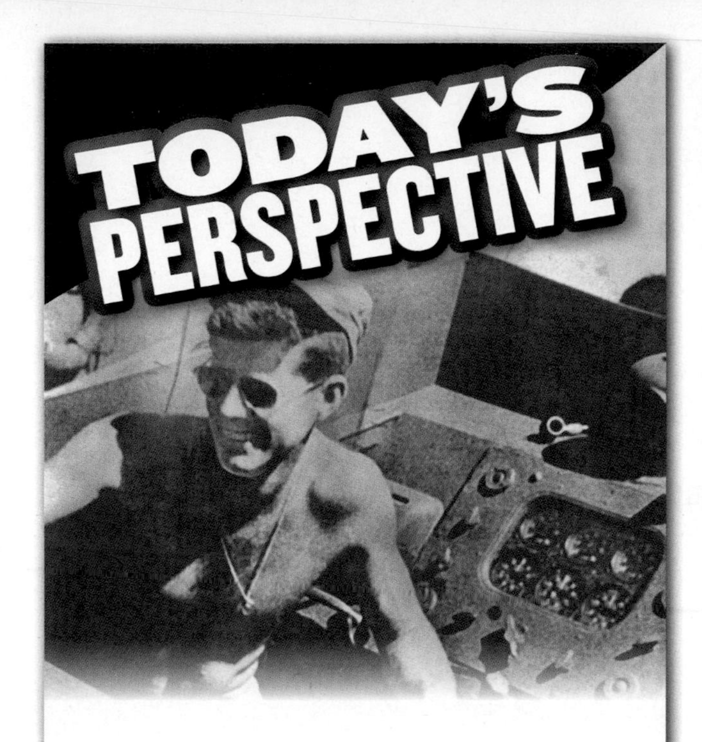

TODAY'S PERSPECTIVE

In August 1943, 26-year-old John F. Kennedy was commander of torpedo boat *PT-109* in the South Pacific during World War II. When the Japanese destroyer *Amagiri* rammed *PT-109*, Kennedy and other survivors were thrown into the water. Only Kennedy's remarkable heroism led them to safety. His status as a war hero contributed to his successful rise in politics, but the collision with *Amagiri* made an old back injury worse. As a result, he was required to wear a large, stiff back brace for the rest of his life. Some researchers have concluded that because of the brace, Kennedy could not slump forward for protection after he was shot the first time. Instead, Kennedy sat up with his head exposed, providing Oswald with a clean shot.

As the anchor of *CBS Evening News* between 1962 and 1981, Walter Cronkite reported on a wide range of historic events, including the Kennedy assassination.

a tube in the president's windpipe to help him breathe. He also placed tubes in Kennedy's right ankle to supply blood and other fluids. A chest tube was inserted to drain accumulating blood. When Kennedy's personal doctor, George Burkley, entered the trauma room, he quickly saw that the president's condition was hopeless. Kennedy lost his struggle for life at 1:00 p.m. CST.

Meanwhile, doctors across the hall worked to save Governor Connally. The governor's wounds were serious but not life threatening. He endured two surgeries and survived his ordeal.

At 2:38 p.m. eastern standard time (1:38 CST), CBS news anchor Walter Cronkite, visibly saddened, announced to anxious Americans that their president had died.

A FIRSTHAND LOOK AT
NEWS COVERAGE OF THE ASSASSINATION

The assassination of John F. Kennedy was a major news event. The nation was shocked as television and radio presenters announced Kennedy's death. See page 60 for a link to watch legendary news anchor Walter Cronkite announce the assassination on CBS.

Manhunt

Within minutes of the sniper attack, squad cars gathered at Dealey Plaza. As the motorcade sped toward the hospital, police officers swarmed into the book depository. Officers outside interviewed eyewitnesses to the attack. Several witnesses said the shots had come from the book depository. A few of them pinpointed the

Police officers quickly began searching the book depository for evidence. One item they found was this paper bag, which was believed to have been used to carry a rifle into the building.

southeastern window on the sixth floor as the shooter's perch. They described the sniper as a slender white male in his twenties and of average height. Two officers were stationed at the book depository's front door so no one could get in or out.

At about the same time, seven blocks east of the book depository, a Dallas Transit Company bus was caught in the traffic jam caused by the motorcade. The bus driver heard a man banging on the bus door and opened it to let him inside. Mary Bledsoe, one of the bus's passengers, recognized the man as Lee Harvey Oswald. She had briefly rented a home to him the previous month but

Lee Harvey Oswald met and married Marina Nikolayevna Prusakova while living in the Soviet Union.

had asked him to leave. He made her feel uncomfortable. Fifteen minutes later, the bus had made little progress. Oswald and another passenger got off and began walking.

At 12:45, Oswald's wife, Marina, heard news of the assassination and the description of the sniper. Her heart sank. Lee and Marina were separated, so they did not live in the same house. However, Lee had stopped to visit the night before and gone into the garage. Marina wondered if he had retrieved the gun that he kept there.

Across town, cab driver William Whaley picked up Lee Harvey Oswald at the Greyhound bus station. Oswald told Whaley that he needed to go to the Oak Cliff section of Dallas, south of the Trinity River. At the same time, police dispatcher Murray Jackson coincidentally directed officers to Oak Cliff. The presence of so many officers at Dealey Plaza had left other parts of the city shorthanded. As patrolman J. D. Tippit drove toward Oak Cliff, the investigation on Dealey Plaza heated up. A witness named Howard Brennan described the gunman to Agent Sorrels, saying he could positively identify him. Police officers mistakenly believed the gunman was still in the book depository.

Televised coverage of the unfolding drama had begun. Earlene Roberts of Oak Cliff was adjusting her television to watch the news reports as one of her boarders rushed in, went to his room, and shut the door. The boarder was Lee Harvey Oswald. Oswald put on his coat and slipped his revolver inside. He rushed back outside without speaking to his landlady.

Officer J. D. Tippit was just 39 years old when he was shot and killed in his attempt to stop Oswald.

Six minutes later, the investigators at Dealey Plaza discovered the sniper's nest in the southeastern corner of the sixth floor of the book depository. Officers found three bullet **casings** on the floor and a long, brown paper wrapper used to bring the rifle into the building. A short time later, the rifle itself was found among piles of boxes.

Meanwhile, in Oak Cliff, Officer Tippit saw a man who strongly resembled the police description of Kennedy's assassin. It was Lee Harvey Oswald. Tippit eased up alongside Oswald and got out of the car to approach him. Oswald grabbed his revolver, turned, and gunned Tippit down. Then he calmly walked away as a witness used the police radio in Tippit's abandoned car to report the shooting. Moments later, Dallas police sped toward Tenth Street, where Tippit had been slain. They received eyewitness descriptions of Tippit's killer and began their search.

At Dealey Plaza, investigators conducted a roll call of book depository workers. A worker named Lee Harvey Oswald was scheduled to be there, but he was missing. Dallas police and the FBI soon realized that the descriptions of the sniper and J. D. Tippit's killer matched that of Oswald. The manhunt in Oak Cliff intensified. At 1:46, officers at the murder scene in Oak Cliff received word that a man matching Oswald's description had been

Oswald was living at 1026 North Beckley Avenue at the time of the Kennedy assassination.

Members of the press swarmed the police station when Oswald was brought in for questioning.

seen slipping into the Texas Theatre on West Jefferson. In moments, squad cars surrounded the theater. Officers entered and saw Oswald sitting near the back of the theater. They quickly swarmed toward him. Oswald stood, and a struggle for his revolver broke out. Three officers fought him, hoping the loaded gun wouldn't fire. At last, the officers grabbed the revolver, handcuffed Oswald, and led him to the police cruiser.

By 2:02, the police officers arrived at headquarters with Oswald to begin his **interrogation**. At around 2:15, they received shocking news from Washington, D.C.: Oswald had ties to the communist Soviet Union. The assassination had taken on a new and frightening dimension.

A New President

At Parkland Memorial Hospital, doctors who wanted to perform an **autopsy** on the president's body battled with Secret Service agents intent on flying the body to Bethesda Naval Hospital in Maryland. After a tense standoff and angry shouting back and forth, Kennedy's corpse was driven to Love Field and brought aboard Air Force One. On the plane immediately before takeoff, Lyndon Johnson was sworn in as the nation's 36th president. Jacqueline Kennedy stood at his side, still wearing her bloodstained suit.

Lyndon Johnson

As the new president, Lyndon Johnson carried on many of Kennedy's policies. For example, he helped pass the Civil Rights Act of 1964. The act struck down school **segregation**, which had persisted in the South for a decade after the landmark *Brown v. Board of Education* case made it illegal. Johnson also had plenty of ideas of his own. His Great Society program increased access to medical care and education. It also addressed a host of problems plaguing American cities.

Johnson faced difficulties in his presidency as well. After expanding America's role in the Vietnam War, he met with strong antiwar protests across the nation. Facing a nation of voters who blamed him for the war, Johnson chose not to run for reelection in 1968.

CHAPTER 3
INVESTIGATING OSWALD

Lee Harvey Oswald's mug shot reveals injuries from his scuffle with police at the Texas Theatre.

THE SHOOTINGS OF JOHN F. Kennedy, John Connally, and J. D. Tippit were Oswald's first brush with the law. But the Dallas FBI office had already become familiar with Oswald the previous year. After spending time in the Soviet Union, Oswald had returned to the United States with his wife, Marina. Here, Oswald passed out leaflets supporting the communist revolution of Fidel Castro in Cuba. Because of these ties to communism, Oswald was investigated by FBI agent James Hosty. However, Oswald was never charged with a crime.

James Hosty (front) later expressed his regret that he had been unable to stop Oswald in his earlier investigation.

Gathering Evidence

Upon Oswald's arrest for the shootings, experienced Dallas police interrogator J. W. Fritz was brought in to conduct the first interview. He quickly learned that Oswald lived at 1026 North Beckley Avenue in Oak Cliff, rather than at the home where his wife resided. Oswald had a false ID in his wallet with the **alias** A. J. Hidell. He informed Captain Fritz that he had "picked it up in New Orleans," where he had previously lived.

Detectives were dispatched to 1026 North Beckley. They found that Oswald had registered under the name O. H. Lee and that he was renting a very small single room. The investigation was now picking up steam. Agent Hosty arrived and joined in the Oswald interrogation. However, his presence seemed to irritate Oswald. Hosty asked questions about Oswald's communist ties, and Oswald became angry and less cooperative. Fritz calmed him and changed the subject. Oswald answered questions about his youth and schooling. He told Fritz he had dropped out of school to join the marines. He also had earned "an award for marksmanship." However, he denied currently owning a rifle or shooting Kennedy, Connally, and Tippit. When Oswald was searched minutes later, bullets were discovered in his pants pockets. A short time later, a witness to the Tippit murder, named Helen Markham, identified Oswald in a lineup.

Lee Harvey Oswald used this gun and these bullets to kill Officer J. D. Tippit.

A photograph revealed that Oswald owned guns exactly like the ones that had killed President Kennedy and J. D. Tippit.

Detectives secured a search **warrant** for Oswald's room on North Beckley. They cleaned the room out. Everything became evidence. Another team visited Marina Oswald in Irving, Texas, collected evidence, and escorted her to the police station for questioning. It was 6:16 p.m. when Captain Fritz came to the crime lab and asked Lieutenant Carl Day to bring the rifle from the book depository downstairs. Marina Oswald agreed that it looked similar to the gun her husband owned, but said she could not be absolutely certain.

Additional evidence would soon leave no doubt that Oswald had fired the rifle. Cotton fibers matching those from Oswald's shirt were found on the rifle's wooden stock. Oswald's palm print was on the rifle barrel. His fingerprints were found on the boxes that had been arranged to make the sniper's nest and on the brown paper wrapper the gunman had used to transport the rifle into the book depository. Experts examined the bullet fragments found in SS-100-X and a nearly whole bullet found on Governor Connally's gurney. They concluded that all of the bullets came from the assassin's rifle recovered from the book depository. Tests showed Oswald had gunshot **residue** on his hands. This proved that he had recently fired a weapon.

Records revealed that the mail-order rifle had been shipped to "A. Hidell" at P.O. Box 2915 on March 20, 1963. This matched the name on Oswald's false ID. In addition, the order form for the gun showed a signature in Oswald's handwriting, and the post office box had been registered to Oswald at the time the gun was delivered. The revolver used to kill Tippit had been shipped to the same address. Finally, backyard photographs taken by Oswald's wife showed Oswald holding the same rifle and

A FIRSTHAND LOOK AT
THE ZAPRUDER FILM

Investigators viewed Abraham Zapruder's film of the Kennedy assassination countless times to extract information about the murder. It confirmed the physical evidence in the case and allowed investigators to figure out the precise timing of the shots fired on the motorcade. See page 60 for a link to view the film online.

revolver in April 1963. The mountain of evidence made it clear that Oswald had purchased and recently fired the weapons used to kill Kennedy and Tippit.

Abraham Zapruder's film of the assassination lent further weight to the evidence piling up against Oswald. The reactions of the limousine's passengers and the injuries to Connally and Kennedy matched up with frame-by-frame evidence from the Zapruder film. Both pointed to a sniper attack from the book depository. None of the evidence, however, could explain the reason for Oswald's actions.

"Ozzie Rabbit"

Detectives searching the items taken from Oswald's room were alarmed by the suspect's collection of Russian-language newspapers. The discovery seemed to defy explanation. Some wondered whether Oswald might be a Soviet spy. They set about retracing the path

Abraham Zapruder's camera (above) captured the carefully examined video footage of the Kennedy assassination.

Lee Harvey Oswald's difficult childhood helped set him on a dark path.

that brought him to the sniper's nest. They found that Oswald had had a troubled childhood. His father died two months before Oswald was born. Oswald's mother, Marguerite, was forced to put Lee and his two older brothers in an orphanage because she did not have enough money to care for them. Oswald spent more than a year living in the orphanage before his mother was able to bring him and his brothers back home.

Marguerite Oswald took on odd jobs to support the family, leaving Lee to himself. His brothers were several years older and weren't around to look after him. Lee drifted into his own world. He formed no lasting friendships with other children. When his mother moved the family from Texas to New York, classmates made fun of

YESTERDAY'S HEADLINES

In September 1959, just before his 20th birthday, Lee Harvey Oswald deserted from the U.S. Marines. The event, unthinkable at the height of the Cold War, was reported in the *Miami News*. Oswald's desertion also got the attention of the FBI, which began to keep a file on his activities. The FBI never shared that knowledge with Dallas police prior to the assassination.

Lee's western clothing. He stopped going to school and often got in trouble. The family continued to move around as Marguerite looked for work. By the time Lee left school to join the marines, he had moved 22 times in 17 years.

In the marines, Oswald became an expert marksman. He kept to himself and was not popular with other marines. Because he was small and immature, some of the men ridiculed him by calling him "Ozzie Rabbit." Oswald began to argue with officers. He considered himself more intelligent than they were and thought they were not fit to give him orders. Increasingly, his thoughts turned to the Soviet Union. He liked the ideas of the country's communist government. In September 1959, Oswald left the marines, moved to the Soviet Union, and tried unsuccessfully to become a Soviet citizen. He hoped to attend Moscow University but instead ended up working at a factory. He grew bored and dissatisfied with his surroundings once again, and returned to the United States in 1962 with his Russian wife, Marina.

Back in the United States, Oswald bounced from one job to another. His marriage began to fall apart. Shortly after he purchased the rifle used in the Kennedy assassination, he tried to shoot former U.S. Army officer General Edwin Walker, narrowly missing. However, Oswald was not linked to Walker's attempted murder until the rifle was tested during the investigation of the Kennedy assassination.

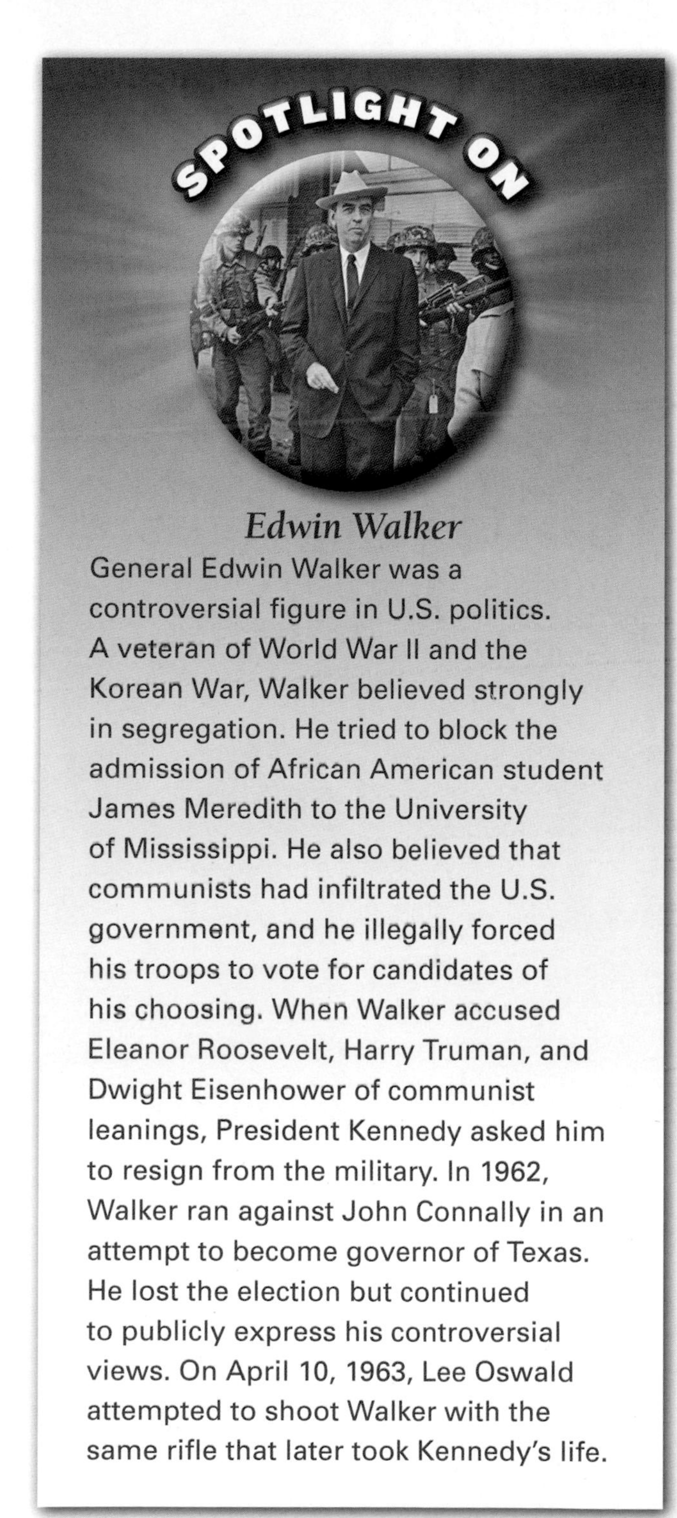

Edwin Walker

General Edwin Walker was a controversial figure in U.S. politics. A veteran of World War II and the Korean War, Walker believed strongly in segregation. He tried to block the admission of African American student James Meredith to the University of Mississippi. He also believed that communists had infiltrated the U.S. government, and he illegally forced his troops to vote for candidates of his choosing. When Walker accused Eleanor Roosevelt, Harry Truman, and Dwight Eisenhower of communist leanings, President Kennedy asked him to resign from the military. In 1962, Walker ran against John Connally in an attempt to become governor of Texas. He lost the election but continued to publicly express his controversial views. On April 10, 1963, Lee Oswald attempted to shoot Walker with the same rifle that later took Kennedy's life.

CHAPTER 4

SORTING OUT THE TRUTH

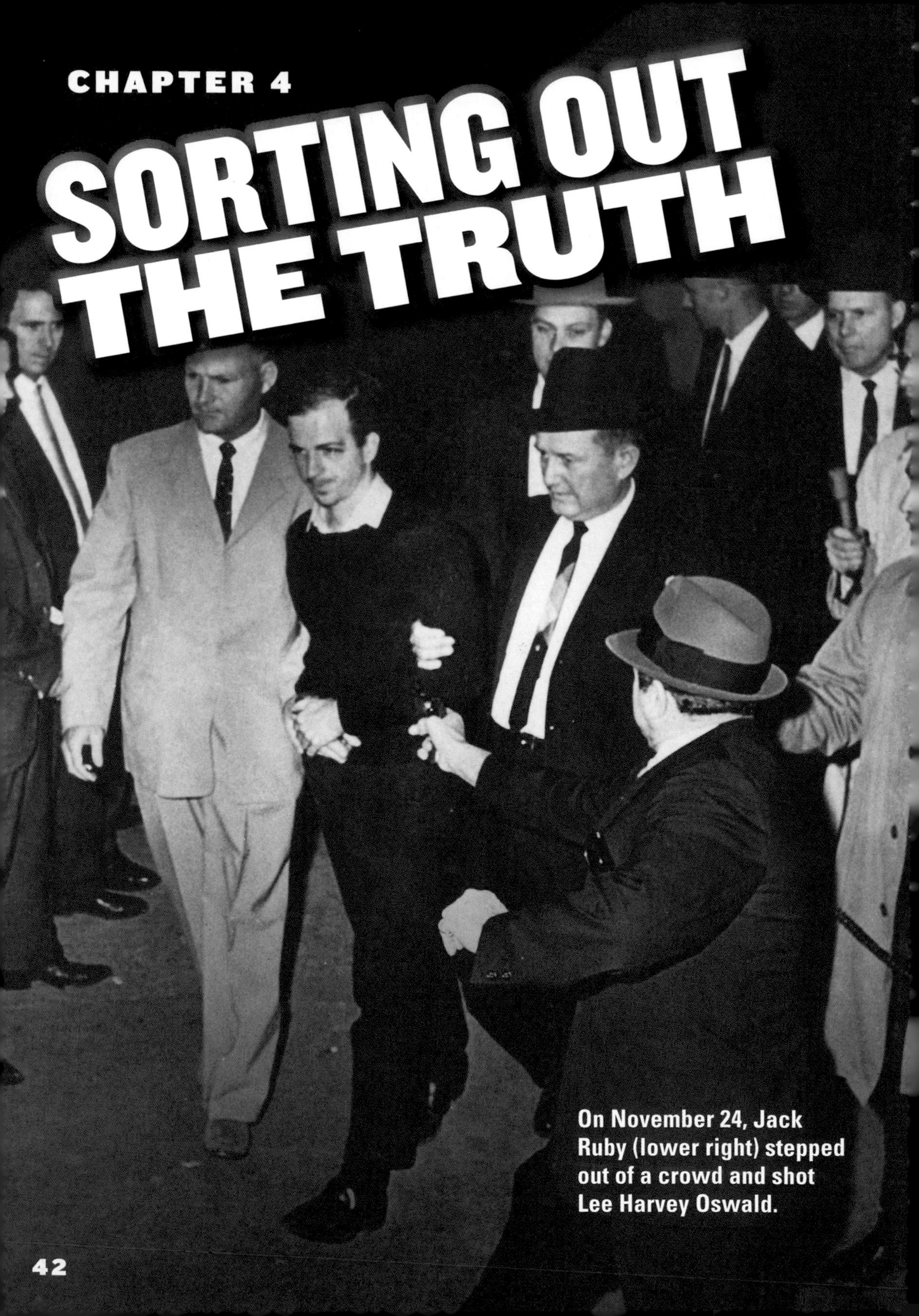

On November 24, Jack Ruby (lower right) stepped out of a crowd and shot Lee Harvey Oswald.

AFTER TWO DAYS OF INTENSIVE questioning, Oswald was to be moved from the Dallas police station to the county jail. As the nation watched the transfer on network television, and a group of people gathered to watch in person, a Dallas nightclub owner named Jack Ruby stepped from the crowd and shot Oswald at close range, killing him. Oswald's long, strange journey was over. He was only 24 years old.

Huge crowds of spectators gathered in Washington, D.C., to mourn the president's death.

With the nation still reeling from the Kennedy assassination, Oswald's murder added to the confusion. Some believed Oswald's connections to communism meant he was a spy. His murder now added to their suspicions.

Mourning

On Saturday, November 23, Kennedy's body was brought to the East Room of the White House. Family members, close friends, members of Congress, and the cabinet came to pay their respects. Outside, a large crowd of mourners stood in steady rain in Lafayette Park, in remembrance of the president.

Sunday, November 24, the nation mourned publicly. More than a quarter million people watched the horse-drawn cart bearing Kennedy's casket travel down Pennsylvania Avenue to the Capitol Rotunda for a public viewing. Mourners in a line more than 10 miles (16 km) long passed by the casket to pay their respects over the next 18 hours. Leaders from around the world soon arrived in Washington, D.C., for Monday's state funeral. The funeral provided closure, but few answers, to the tragedy in Dallas.

YESTERDAY'S HEADLINES

President Kennedy's televised funeral procession was enormous. More than one million mourners lined the route from the Capitol to the White House, and onward to St. Matthew's Cathedral and Arlington National Cemetery. As Kennedy's casket was carried from the cathedral, three-year-old John F. Kennedy Jr. saluted his father's coffin. Kennedy was buried at Arlington exactly two weeks after he had visited the cemetery to pay his respects to America's fallen heroes on Veterans Day.

A VIEW FROM ABROAD

Most nations were shocked by the events in Dallas. Ninety-two countries sent 220 representatives to Kennedy's state funeral. However, reactions varied sharply from one nation to another. The Soviet Union was thrown into a panic. Kennedy had been willing to reach diplomatic solutions to ease tensions between the Soviet Union and the United States. Relatively little was known of his successor, Lyndon Johnson, and how he would handle U.S.-Soviet relations.

Some nations seemed to celebrate the president's death. A newspaper in China, a communist country, published a disrespectful cartoon of Kennedy, with the caption, "Kennedy bites the dust!"

Setting the Record Straight

One week after Kennedy's death, President Lyndon Johnson established a **commission** to investigate the assassination. The committee of seven was led by Chief Justice Earl Warren. The investigation was conducted in a series of closed sessions. After about 10 months, the commission presented its report to President Johnson on September 24, 1964.

The commission's findings and methods soon became controversial. It concluded that Lee Harvey Oswald had acted alone in assassinating President Kennedy. The commission's 889-page report closely examined Oswald's history. His three years in the Soviet Union led to intense speculation that he was part of a

The Warren Commission included future president Gerald Ford (far left) and Chief Justice Earl Warren (center).

larger **conspiracy**. There were rumors that Oswald had received payments from mysterious sources and that he possessed detailed records of Castro supporters. The commission determined that none of the rumors were true, but some people remained skeptical. They argued that the commission was covering up evidence.

Almost as controversial was the commission's conclusion that Oswald had fired only three shots. According to its findings, the first shot missed, the second bullet struck both Kennedy and Connally, and the third hit Kennedy in the head. The second bullet caused all of Connally's wounds. It had been recovered from Connally's gurney nearly intact. The commission

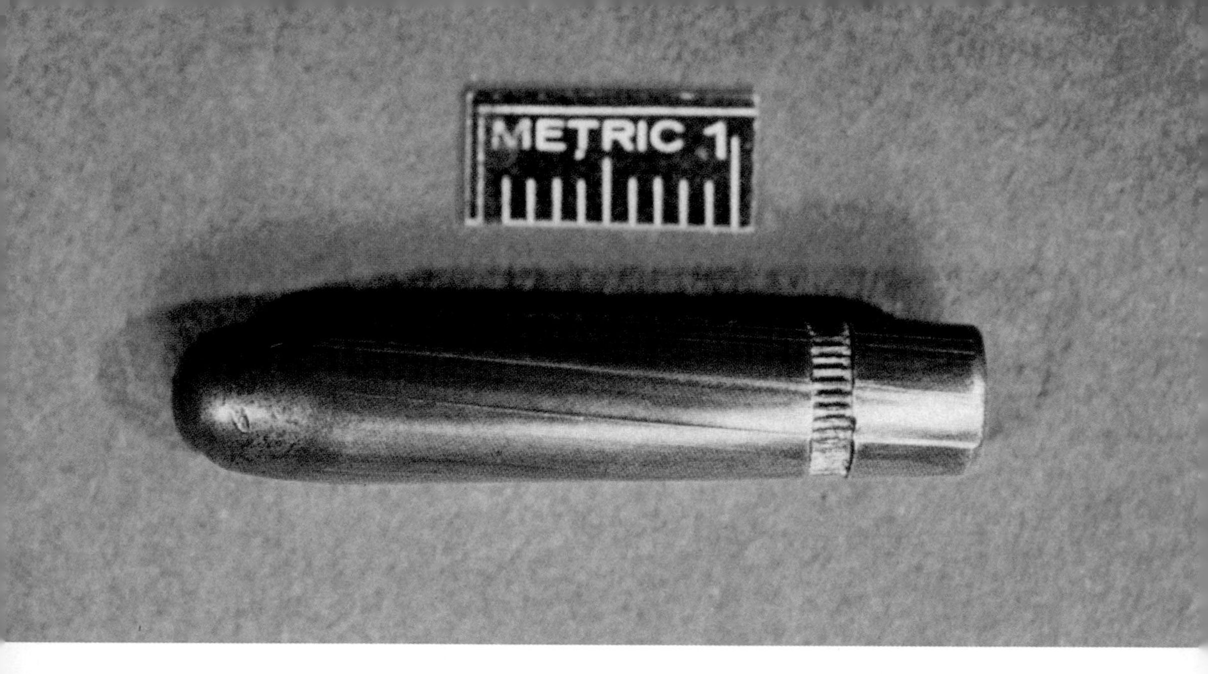

This bullet was discovered on Governor Connally's gurney. The Warren Commission determined that it had struck both Kennedy and Connally.

eventually concluded that the bullet had entered Kennedy's back, brushed his spine and the top of his right lung, and exited below his Adam's apple, hitting the knot of his tie. The bullet then began to tumble from side to side. As a result, it created a larger entrance wound than normal when it hit the governor's back. When it exited, it left a wound 2 inches (5 centimeters) wide in the right side of Connally's chest and then passed through his wrist before sticking in his left thigh.

This theory that a single bullet hit both Kennedy and Connally was controversial from the start. It was supported by only four of the committee's seven members. However, the theory was a necessary part of the commission's argument that Oswald acted alone. Close examination of the Zapruder film shows that Kennedy was struck around frame 220. Connally was

A FIRSTHAND LOOK AT THE WARREN COMMISSION REPORT

The Warren Commission Report provides a thorough analysis of the Kennedy assassination. However, its findings were, and remain, controversial. See page 60 for a link to read the report online.

struck at frame 240. Zapruder's camera averaged 18.3 frames per second. It would not have been possible for Oswald to fire two shots from his rifle in little more than one second, so the bullet must have struck both Kennedy and Connally. Some believe that the timing is instead evidence of a second gunman. However, the gunshot wounds examined in the autopsy support the commission's findings.

Investigators carefully examined every frame of the Zapruder film as they attempted to solve the mysteries of the assassination.

In the interest of protecting witnesses, all of the commission's records were sealed for 75 years. The 1966 Freedom of Information Act and later the 1992 President John F. Kennedy Assassination Records Collection Act made it possible to access nearly all of the commission's records. Dissatisfaction with the commission's findings and methods persisted. But in 1968 and again in 1975, federal government investigations upheld the findings of the Warren Commission Report.

In 1976, in response to the public release of the Zapruder film and countless documentaries about the assassination, the House of Representatives formed a committee to reconsider the evidence. Relying on

The House Select Committee on Assassinations conducted another detailed investigation into the Kennedy assassination in 1976.

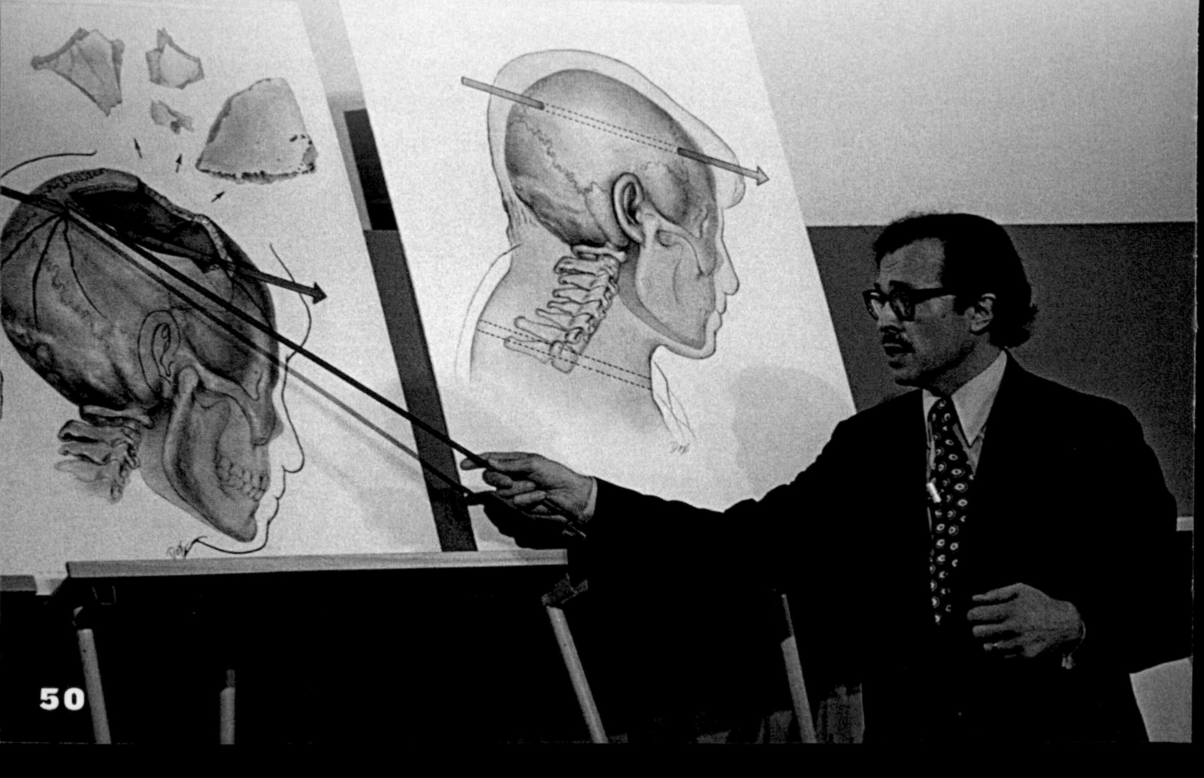

Mourners gathered at President Kennedy's grave at Arlington National Cemetery near Washington, D.C.

controversial evidence, the House Select Committee on Assassinations (HSCA) concluded that Oswald likely acted as part of a conspiracy. However, the HSCA made no specific claims about the identities of Oswald's partners. It agreed with the Warren Commission Report that all of the wounds Kennedy and Connally received came from bullets fired by Oswald.

Half a century after Lee Harvey Oswald shocked a nation, John F. Kennedy's assassination remains a controversial topic. People are still fascinated by Kennedy's legacy and wonder how history would have been different had he not been killed.

MAP OF THE EVENTS

What Happened Where?

Dallas Love Field

D A L

Texas School Book Depository

Lee Harvey Oswald was an employee at the Texas School Book Depository. Recognizing that President Kennedy's motorcade would pass the building's view, Oswald chose it as the site of his sniper nest.

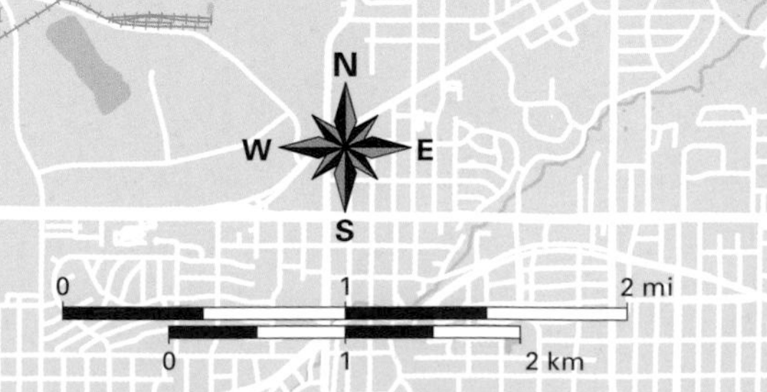

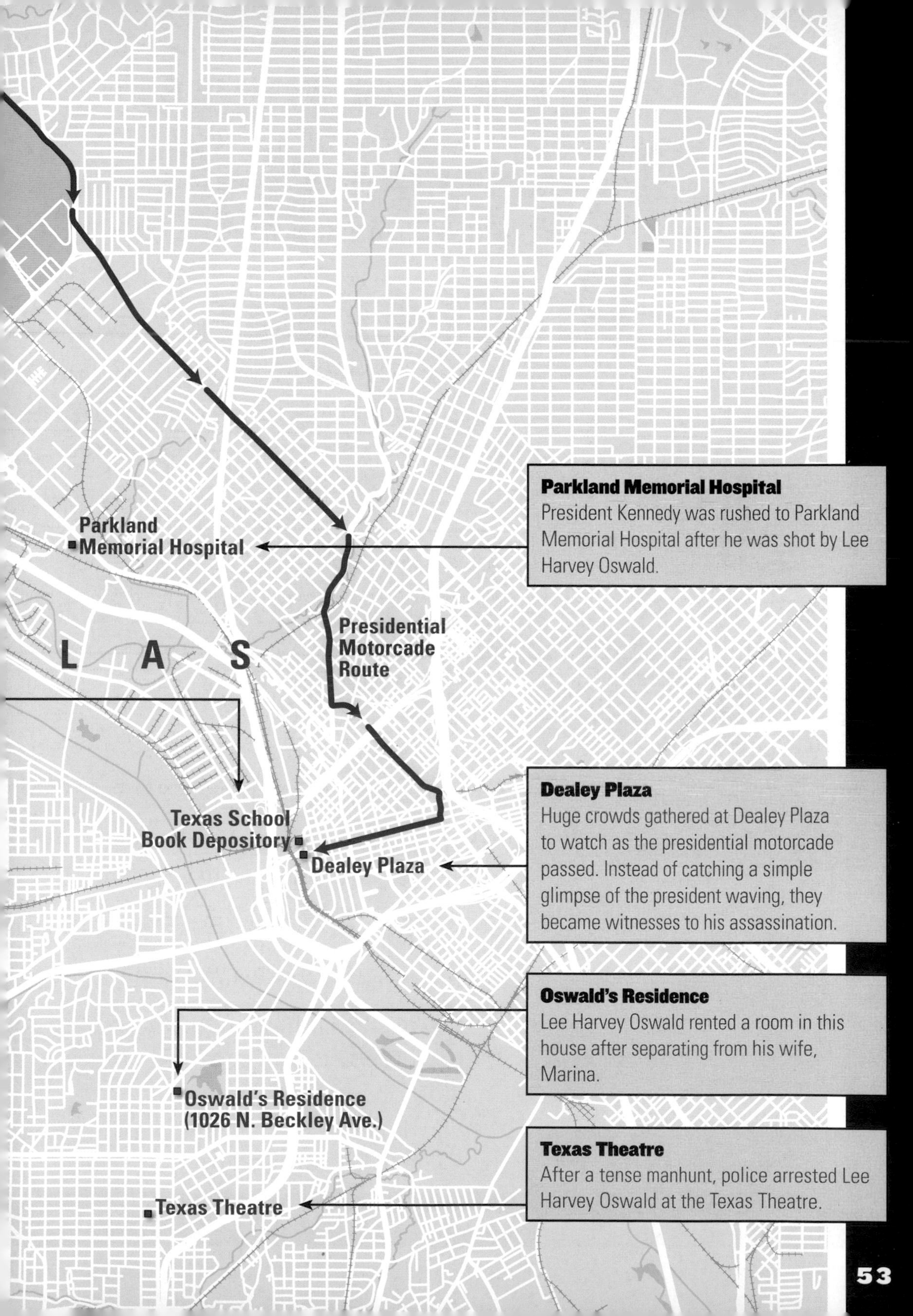
Parkland Memorial Hospital
Presidential Motorcade Route
L A S
Texas School Book Depository
Dealey Plaza
Oswald's Residence (1026 N. Beckley Ave.)
Texas Theatre
Parkland Memorial Hospital
President Kennedy was rushed to Parkland Memorial Hospital after he was shot by Lee Harvey Oswald.
Dealey Plaza
Huge crowds gathered at Dealey Plaza to watch as the presidential motorcade passed. Instead of catching a simple glimpse of the president waving, they became witnesses to his assassination.
Oswald's Residence
Lee Harvey Oswald rented a room in this house after separating from his wife, Marina.
Texas Theatre
After a tense manhunt, police arrested Lee Harvey Oswald at the Texas Theatre.

THE STORY CONTINUES

Presidential Protection

U.S. presidents no longer ride in convertible limousines.

The Warren Commission Report concluded that the Secret Service's poor planning had contributed to the tragedy in Dallas. As a result, future presidents were given stronger protection. The presidential limousine was outfitted with a permanent bulletproof roof and bulletproof windows. In addition, Secret Service procedures and training were improved.

PRESIDENT OBAMA'S PRESIDENTIAL CAR

Despite these measures, U.S. presidents have continued to be targets of assassins. On March 30, 1981, President Ronald Reagan spoke at an event at the Washington Hilton Hotel. His limousine waited just 30 feet (9 m) from the exit. As Reagan made that short walk, a man named John Hinckley Jr. fired six shots from his revolver. The first struck White House press secretary James Brady in the head, permanently disabling him. The sixth struck Reagan, lodging in his lung. The quick reaction of Secret Service agents prevented further catastrophe, and Reagan made a full recovery. However, the shooting proved that even with the best security, it can be difficult to defend one of the world's most powerful leaders from those intent on doing harm.

Secret Service agents tackled John Hinckley Jr. after he attempted to assassinate President Reagan.

IS A CUSTOM-MADE ARMORED CADILLAC.

INFLUENTIAL INDIVIDUALS

Lyndon Johnson

John F. Kennedy

Earl Warren (1891–1974) was the chief justice of the Supreme Court of the United States. He served as chairman of the commission that investigated the Kennedy assassination.

Lyndon Johnson (1908–1973) served as vice president under John F. Kennedy. After Kennedy's assassination, he was sworn in as the 36th president of the United States.

Jack Ruby (1911–1967) was a nightclub owner in Dallas. He shot and killed Lee Harvey Oswald in the basement of the Dallas police station.

John F. Kennedy (1917–1963) was the 35th president of the United States. He founded the Peace Corps, supported NASA, and was a supporter of civil rights reform. He was assassinated on November 22, 1963.

John Connally (1917–1993) was the governor of Texas. He was critically injured in the attack on Kennedy.

Jacqueline Kennedy (1929–1994) was the wife of John F. Kennedy. She was riding next to him when he was shot.

Lee Harvey Oswald (1939–1963) was the sniper who shot President Kennedy and Governor Connally from a sixth-floor window of the Texas School Book Depository on Dealey Plaza in Dallas.

Marina Oswald (1941–) was Lee Harvey Oswald's wife. Lee and Marina were living separately at the time of the assassination.

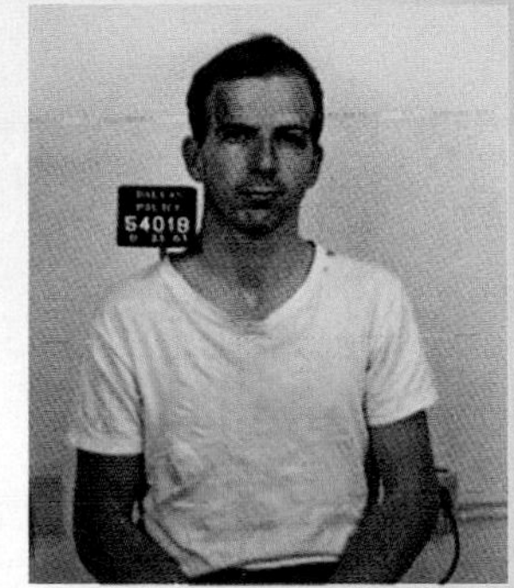

Lee Harvey Oswald

TIMELINE

1963

April
President Kennedy's aides begin planning his appearance in Texas.

April 10
Lee Harvey Oswald attempts to assassinate General Edwin Walker.

October
Oswald begins working at the Texas School Book Depository.

November 15
The Secret Service and Dallas Police Department finalize President Kennedy's motorcade route.

1963

November 24
Kennedy's body lies in state at the Capitol Rotunda; Jack Ruby shoots Oswald.

November 25
Kennedy is buried at Arlington National Cemetery.

November 29
President Johnson establishes the Warren Commission.

November 22, 1963

11:55 a.m. CST
The presidential motorcade leaves the airport.

12:30 p.m. CST
Kennedy is fatally wounded and Governor John Connally is critically injured in a sniper attack.

1:00 p.m. CST
Kennedy is declared dead at Parkland Memorial Hospital.

1:15 p.m. CST
Oswald guns down Dallas police officer J. D. Tippit.

1:46 p.m. CST
Oswald is captured at the Texas Theatre.

2:38 p.m. CST
Lyndon Johnson is sworn in as president aboard Air Force One.

11:00 p.m. EST
An autopsy of Kennedy's body is performed at Bethesda Naval Hospital.

1964

September 24
The Warren Commission Report is presented to President Johnson.

1976–1979

The HSCA reexamines the Kennedy assassination under intense public pressure.

Primary sources provide firsthand evidence about a topic. Witnesses to a historical event create primary sources. They include autobiographies, newspaper reports of the time, oral histories, photographs, and memoirs. A secondary source analyzes primary sources, and is one step or more removed from the event. Secondary sources include textbooks, encyclopedias, and commentaries. To view the following primary and secondary sources, go to www.factsfornow.scholastic.com. Enter the keywords **Assassination of John F. Kennedy** and look for the Living History logo.

The Motorcade's Route The *Dallas Times Herald* published a detailed description of President Kennedy's planned route days before his arrival in Dallas. The publication of the route drew people to the event but also allowed Oswald to plan his attack.

News Coverage of the Assassination The world reacted with shock as news reports of Kennedy's assassination began to appear. CBS's Walter Cronkite delivered a televised report of the tragic news that has become one of the most famous news broadcasts of all time.

The Warren Commission Report The Warren Commission, led by Chief Justice Earl Warren, conducted a detailed investigation into the Kennedy assassination. Its conclusions were controversial but are generally accepted as the most accurate report of the events.

The Zapruder Film Abraham Zapruder, a Kennedy supporter who visited Dealey Plaza to catch a glimpse of the president, recorded what has become the only video footage of the assassination. Zapruder's film was an important resource for investigators attempting to make sense of the shooting.

Books

Kallen, Stuart A. *The John F. Kennedy Assassination*. Detroit: Lucent Books, 2009.

Mara, Wil. *John F. Kennedy*. New York: Marshall Cavendish Benchmark, 2010.

Sandler, Martin W. *Kennedy Through the Lens: How Photography and Television Revealed and Shaped an Extraordinary Leader*. New York: Walker & Co., 2011.

Visit this Scholastic Web site for more information on the assassination of John F. Kennedy:
www.factsfornow.scholastic.com
Enter the keywords Assassination of John F. Kennedy

GLOSSARY

alias (AY-lee-uhs) a false name, especially one used by a criminal

autopsy (AW-tahp-see) an examination performed on a dead person to find the cause of death

casings (KAY-singz) the outer parts of bullets that are left behind when a gun is fired

commission (kuh-MISH-uhn) a group of people who meet to solve a particular problem or do certain tasks

communism (KAHM-yuh-niz-uhm) a way of organizing the economy of a country so that all land, property, businesses, and resources belong to the government or community, and the profits are shared by all

conspiracy (kuhn-SPIR-uh-see) a secret plan made by two or more people to do something illegal or harmful

counterfeiting (KOUN-ter-fit-ing) making something that is fake but looks almost exactly like the real thing, as in counterfeit money

gurney (GUR-nee) a wheeled cot or stretcher

interrogation (in-ter-uh-GAY-shuhn) detailed questioning

motorcade (MOH-tur-kade) a group of cars traveling together, often to transport an important person

residue (REZ-i-doo) what is left after something burns up or evaporates

segregation (seg-ruh-GAY-shuhn) the act of separating people based on race, gender, or other factors

warrant (WOR-uhnt) an official document that gives permission for something, such as searching or arresting someone

Page numbers in *italics* indicate illustrations.

ABOUT THE AUTHOR

Peter Benoit earned a degree in mathematics at Skidmore College. He is an educator and poet. He has written more than four dozen books for Scholastic/Children's Press on topics including disasters, Native Americans, ecosystems, the *Titanic*, the electoral college, and the 2012 election. He has also written several books on crucial moments in American history and books on ancient Greece and ancient Rome. Benoit resides in Greenwich, New York.